Congressional
Research
Service

Hydropower:
Federal and Nonfederal Investment

Kelsi Bracmort
Specialist in Agricultural Conservation and Natural Resources Policy

Charles V. Stern
Specialist in Natural Resources Policy

Adam Vann
Legislative Attorney

June 26, 2012

Congressional Research Service
7-5700
www.crs.gov
R42579

CRS Report for Congress
Prepared for Members and Committees of Congress

Summary

Congress is examining numerous energy sources to determine their contribution to the nation's energy portfolio and the federal role in supporting these sources. Hydropower, the use of flowing water to produce electricity, is one such source. Conventional hydropower accounted for approximately 6% of total U.S. net electricity generation in 2010.

Hydropower has advantages and disadvantages as an energy source. Its advantages include its status as a continuous, or baseload, power source that releases minimal air pollutants during power generation relative to fossil fuels. Some of its disadvantages, depending on the type of hydropower plant, include high initial capital costs, ecosystem disruption, and reduced generation during low water years and seasons.

Hydropower project ownership can be categorized as federal or nonfederal. The bulk of federal projects are owned and managed by the Bureau of Reclamation and the U.S. Army Corps of Engineers. Nonfederal projects are licensed and overseen by the Federal Energy Regulatory Commission (FERC).

Considered by many to be an established energy source, hydropower is not always discussed alongside clean or renewable energy sources in the ongoing energy debate. However, hydropower proponents argue that hydropower is cleaner than some conventional energy sources, and point to recent findings that additional hydropower capacity could help the United States reach proposed energy, economic, and environmental goals. Others argue that the expansion of hydropower in the form of numerous small hydropower projects could have environmental impacts and regulatory concerns similar to those of existing large projects.

Congress faces several issues as it determines how hydropower fits into a changing energy and economic landscape. For example, existing large hydropower infrastructure is aging; many of the nation's hydropower generators and dams are over 30 years old. Proposed options to address this concern include increasing federal funding, utilizing alternative funding, privatizing federally owned dams, and encouraging additional small-capacity generators, among other options. Additionally, whether to significantly expand or encourage expansion of hydropower is likely to require congressional input due to the uncertainty surrounding the clean and renewable energy portfolio within power markets. Potential expansion of hydropower projects could take place by improving efficiency at existing projects or by building new projects, or both. Congressional support for this approach is evident in the House passage of the Bureau of Reclamation Small Conduit Hydropower Development and Rural Jobs Act of 2012 (H.R. 2842). Senate activity on this matter includes the Hydropower Improvement Act of 2011 (S. 629), which proposes to establish a grants program for increased hydropower production, and to amend the Federal Power Act (FPA) to authorize FERC to exempt electric power generation facilities on federal lands from the act's requirements, among other things. Another issue is the rate at which FERC issues licenses for nonfederal projects, which is slower than some find ideal. The licensing process can be delayed significantly as stakeholders and the approximately dozen federal and state agencies involved give their input. FERC responded by developing a more streamlined licensing process in 2003. Still, some object to "mandatory conditions" that federal agencies can place on new or renewed hydropower facilities. The 112th Congress has introduced roughly 25 bills regarding hydropower, a quarter of which are state- or site-specific legislation.

Contents

Figures

Appendixes

Contacts

Introduction

Conventional hydropower[1] accounted for nearly 6% (260,203 gigawatt hours) of total net U.S. electricity generation and 7.5% (78 gigawatts) of net summer generating capacity in 2010.[2] The United States has considerable hydropower potential beyond what is already developed.[3] Although there is some interest in increasing the current level of hydropower investment, such investment remains limited, in part because of federal and nonfederal financial constraints, high uncertainty in electricity generation policies and markets (which may dissuade capital investment), and the environmental operating requirements required for hydropower projects. Some hydropower proponents are pursuing policies to reduce what they view as impediments to hydropower development. Other stakeholders prefer that hydropower investments only proceed when they are protective of other interests, including other water users and the aquatic environment and its species.

At issue for Congress is whether, and if so how, to change federal support for hydropower and what priority to give hydropower vis-à-vis other energy investments, and social and environmental concerns. The 112th Congress has introduced over 25 bills dealing with various aspects of hydropower—a quarter of which are state- or site-specific legislation.[4] Some Members of Congress want to provide further support for small hydropower and nonfederal hydropower at federal sites. For example, the House passed the Bureau of Reclamation Small Conduit Hydropower Development and Rural Jobs Act of 2012 (H.R. 2842), which would amend the Reclamation Power Act of 1939 to authorize the Secretary of the Interior to contract for the development of small conduit hydropower (1.5 megawatts or less) at Reclamation facilities; require that power privilege leases be offered first to an irrigation district or water users association operating or receiving water from the applicable work; and exempt small conduit hydropower development from the National Environmental Policy Act of 1969 (NEPA) in select cases, among other things.[5] Also, the Hydropower Improvement Act of 2011 (S. 629) proposes to

---

[1] This report focuses primarily on conventional hydropower. Conventional hydropower refers to the use of dams or impoundments to store water in a reservoir, whereby water released from the reservoir flows through a turbine to generate electricity. It does not include small hydro, low head hydro, or new hydropower technologies. For more information on these technologies, see CRS Report R41089, *Small Hydro and Low-Head Hydro Power Technologies and Prospects*, by Richard J. Campbell.

[2] U.S. Energy Information Administration, *Electric Power Annual 2010*, November 2011, http://www.eia.gov/electricity/annual/. A gigawatt is equal to one thousand megawatts. EIA defines net generation as the amount of gross generation less the electrical energy consumed at the generating station(s) for station service or auxiliaries. Generator capacity is the maximum output that generating equipment can supply to system load, adjusted for ambient conditions.

[3] The U.S. Department of Energy reports that adding power to nonpowered dams has the potential to add 12 gigawatts of new hydropower capacity, with the 100 largest facilities capable of providing 8 gigawatts. U.S. Department of Energy, *An Assessment of Energy Potential at Non-Powered Dams in the United States*, April 2012, http://www1.eere.energy.gov/water/pdfs/npd_report.pdf.

[4] Examples of state- and project-specific legislation includes the Bonneville Unit Clean Hydropower Facilitation Act (S. 499) which would authorize the Secretary of the Interior to facilitate the development of hydroelectric power on the Diamond Fork System of the Central Utah Project. Another example is S. 524, which would terminate certain hydropower reservations relating to Bureau of Land Management patents in Madera County, California.

[5] A lease of power privilege is a contractual right given to a nonfederal entity to use a Bureau of Reclamation facility for electric power generation consistent with Reclamation project purposes. The National Environmental Policy Act of 1969 (NEPA, 42 U.S.C. §§4321-4347) requires that a detailed statement of environmental impacts be prepared for all major federal actions significantly affecting the environment. The exemption of certain projects from NEPA compliance has been a contentious aspect of the hydropower debate. For more information on NEPA, see CRS Report RL33152, The National Environmental Policy Act (NEPA): Background and Implementation, by Linda Luther.

establish a Department of Energy grants program for increased hydropower production, and amends the Federal Power Act (FPA) to authorize the Federal Energy Regulatory Commission (FERC) to exempt electric power generation facilities on federal lands from the act's requirements among other things.

The variety of legislative proposals and stakeholder opinions stems partly from differing views of the benefits and costs of hydropower development. Many have pointed out advantages and drawbacks of conventional hydropower. Cited advantages include its renewable energy status,[6] zero to minimal greenhouse gas emissions during operation, and high operational efficiency. Supporters also note its ability to generally serve as a reliable and flexible domestic energy source. Generally speaking, hydropower generation can be dispatched on relatively short notice, and can supplement shortfalls in generation. However, others note that conventional hydropower has high initial capital costs, can be detrimental to surrounding ecosystems (e.g., fish and wildlife), may not be reliable during low water years and seasons, and may disrupt recreational or scenic values.[7]

The legislative environment for hydropower can be abstruse. Whether the hydropower project investor is a federal or nonfederal entity dictates which laws apply. Several federal government agencies own and operate large hydropower projects, while other agencies administer the process by which nonfederal hydropower projects are built, maintained, and operated. Large federal hydropower projects are managed primarily by the U.S. Department of the Interior's Bureau of Reclamation (hereinafter referred to as Reclamation) and the U.S. Army Corps of Engineers (hereinafter referred to as the Corps). The power from these projects is marketed by the Department of Energy's Power Marketing Administrations (PMAs). FERC regulates investigation, construction, and operations of nonfederal hydropower projects as well as overseeing dam safety for nonfederal projects.

This report explains how the federal government is involved directly in hydropower generation at federal facilities and in the regulation of nonfederal hydropower generation; the focus is on current roles and processes and common concerns and questions about changing those roles.

Background

Most of U.S. hydropower capacity is from conventional hydropower.8 Conventional hydropower plants take three general forms: storage (or impoundment), run-of-river (or diversion), and

---

[6] Some states do not consider hydropower to be a renewable energy source per state guidelines. For example, California does not consider a new hydropower facility an eligible energy resource for its renewable portfolio standard if it will require a new or increased appropriation or diversion of water under certain Division 2, Part 2 of the California water code..

[7] Certain conditions, such as a drought, which reduce water availability may impact the ability of a hydropower plant to generate the amount of electricity intended. There is an ongoing debate about whether and how to consider potential climate change and its impact on hydropower plant operations during the hydropower plant licensing process. For more information, see Joshua H. Viers, "Hydropower Relicensing and Climate Change," *Journal of the American Water Resources Association*, August 2011.

[8] M. J. Sale, U.S. Army Corps of Engineers, Institute for Water Resources, *Outlook for the U.S. Army Corps of Engineers Hydropower Program*, 2011-WRO-P-02, Washington, DC, March 2011, p.1. (Hereinafter referred to as "Corps Hydropower Outlook").

pumped storage.9 A storage plant uses a dam to store enough water in a reservoir so that, when released, it flows through a penstock to a turbine, spinning it, which in turn activates a generator to produce electricity.10 A run-of-river plant directs a portion of a river through a canal or penstock to generate electricity without the need for a reservoir. A pumped storage facility stores energy by pumping water from a lower reservoir to an upper reservoir during off-peak hours; and during periods of higher electricity demand, the water is released to generate electricity.

Conventional hydropower is a significant contributor to the national electric power portfolio.[11] Hydropower produced 6%-9% of total U.S. electric generation between 1998 and 2009, depending on water availability.12 Hydropower accounted for roughly 6% and 9% of the U.S. generation in 2010 and 2011, respectively.13 Hydropower was the largest contributor to renewable electric power generation in 2011, followed by wind, and wood and wood-derived fuels.14 The top hydropower-producing states in 2011 were western states—Washington, Oregon, and California.15

There is an ongoing debate about whether hydropower should be characterized as "renewable." It has historically been characterized as renewable because it is a replenishable resource. More recently, others have asserted that it is not renewable because of its size (e.g., in the case of large-scale projects) and environmental impact, particularly on ecosystems, and in some cases induced evaporation (particularly at reservoirs at low elevations in dry climates) and greenhouse gas emissions during construction. For purposes of this report, hydropower is discussed as renewable because it does not originate from a fossil fuel (i.e., its source is not finite).

The precise number of hydropower projects in the United States is unknown.[16] Different databases yield different results based on selected criteria. **Figure 1** shows the location of both nonfederal (FERC-regulated) hydropower projects and federal hydropower projects. Additionally, 90 nonfederal hydropower projects are licensed to operate at Corps dams, and 28 are licensed to operate at Bureau of Reclamation sites.[17]

---

[9] More information on the types of hydropower plants is available at http://www1.eere.energy.gov/water/hydro_plant_types.html.

[10] A penstock is a closed conduit or pipe for conducting water to the powerhouse.

[11] At one time, hydropower accounted for 40% of U.S. electricity generation. Over time, as other electricity sources expanded, hydropower's share decreased. Other reasons for the decline in electricity generation from hydropower include aging infrastructure, market conditions, environmental and ecosystem concerns, and the fact that large conventional hydropower projects are mostly already developed.

[12] U.S. Energy Information Administration, *Hydropower Has a Long History in the United States*, June 8, 2011, http://www.eia.gov/todayinenergy/detail.cfm?id=2130.

[13] U.S. Energy Information Administration, *Electric Power Monthly*, October 2011, http://www.eia.gov/electricity/monthly/; U.S. Energy Information Administration, *Electric Power Monthly*, December 2011, http://www.eia.doe.gov/cneaf/electricity/epm/epm_sum.html. EIA defines net generation as the amount of gross generation less the electrical energy consumed at the generating station(s) for station service or auxiliaries. Electricity required for pumping at pumped-storage plants is regarded as electricity for station service and is deducted from gross generation.

[14] U.S. Energy Information Administration, *Electricity Data*, February 2012, http://www.eia.gov/electricity/data.cfm#generation.

[15] U.S. Energy Information Administration, *Electric Power Monthly*, February 2012.

[16] This is especially true for nonfederal hydropower projects, as one project could have multiple generating stations.

[17] U.S. Army Corps of Engineers , *U.S. Army Corps of Engineers Civil Works*, 2009, http://www.usace.army.mil/CECW/Documents/cecwm/5_yr1/fy09_5yrplan.pdf; Bureau of Reclamation, *Hydroelectric Powerplants Operated by Others*, 2011, http://www.usbr.gov/power/data/faclothr.html.

The public sector (federal, cooperatives, and municipalities) owns the majority of hydropower capacity, while the private sector (e.g., private utility, private non-utility, and industrial entities) owns the majority of individual hydropower projects. According to a 2006 Idaho National Lab (INL) study, the private sector owns two-thirds of U.S. hydropower plants. However, private plants account for just over 25% of production capacity.[18] Similarly, the public sector owns roughly one-third of the hydropower plants; these plants are responsible for roughly three-quarters of capacity. The federal government tends to own mostly large hydropower (> 30 MW) plants. The private sector and cooperatives tend to own mostly small hydro (1-30 MW) and low power (< 1 MW) plants. Small hydro and low power plants constitute approximately 11% and less than 1% of total hydropower production capacity, respectively. Large hydropower plants are responsible for approximately 89% of total hydropower capacity.[19]

Figure 1. Conventional U.S. Hydropower Projects: Federal and FERC-Regulated

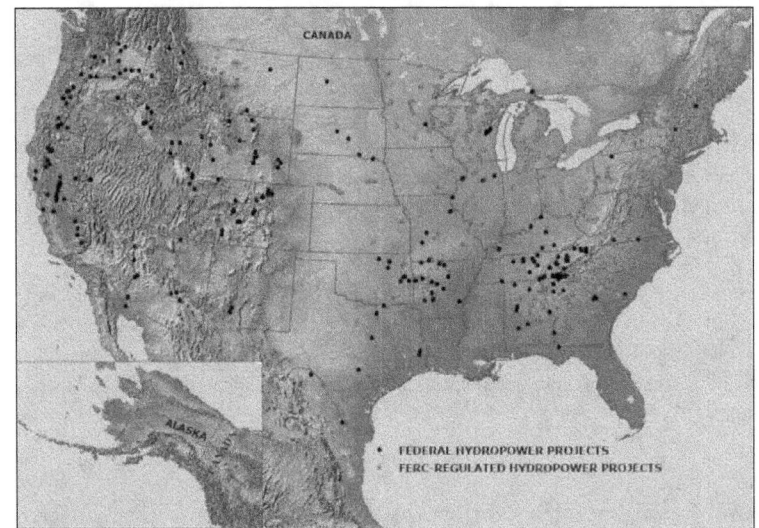

Source: FERC, July 2011.

Notes: According to FERC records, no licenses were issued for projects in Hawaii. However, one exemption was issued, and five projects in Hawaii have been issued preliminary permits.

Federal Hydropower

The federal government owns and operates approximately half of all U.S. hydroelectric generating capacity. This capacity is principally at large multi-purpose dams owned and operated by the Corps or Reclamation. Combined, the Corps and Reclamation operate almost all federal

---

[18] Douglas G. Hall and Kelly S. Reeves, *A Study of United States Hydroelectric Plant Ownership*, Idaho National Laboratory, June 2006, http://hydropower.inel.gov/hydrofacts/pdfs/
a_study_of_united_states_hydroelectric_plant_ownership.pdf. The study categorized hydropower plant ownership in six classes: federal, industrial, cooperative, private utility, private non-utility, and municipal and other nonfederal public.

[19] Ibid.

hydroelectric dam capacity (91% of federal capacity).[20] Other federal entities operating hydroelectric generation facilities include the Tennessee Valley Authority, the Bureau of Indian Affairs, and the International Boundary and Water Commission. Other entities also own facilities that generate hydroelectric power, but they are relatively small. While the electricity generated by these facilities is owned by these federal agencies, the Power Marketing Administrations (PMAs), which are part of the U.S. Department of Energy, are generally responsible for selling and distributing this power.

Federal hydropower capacity varies substantially by state and region. For instance, 90% of all federal capacity is found in 13 states, and the majority of this capacity is in the West.[21] Washington and California contain the greatest federal hydroelectric capacity, while Oregon, Arizona, Montana, and Idaho also have significant federal hydropower capacity. In the East, New York, Georgia, South Carolina, and North Carolina have the most federal capacity.

U.S. Army Corps of Engineers Projects

The Corps' multi-purpose dams are the largest producer of hydropower in the United States. Much of this power generation capacity is concentrated in the Pacific Northwest. The Corps constructed hydropower facilities at many of its water resources projects, beginning in 1925. Its most recent hydroelectric construction project was the R.D. Willis project in Texas, completed in 1989. Today, the Corps owns and operates 353 units at 75 projects, with a total estimated capacity of 25.8 GW, or approximately one-fourth of all national hydropower capacity.[22] These projects generate approximately 70,000 gigawatt hours (GWH) of hydropower annually, with an average gross revenue of $5 billion.[23] Revenues from the sale of this hydropower are deposited into the U.S. Treasury.

Hydropower generating units have a nominal 50-year life expectancy, and many Corps hydropower projects are nearing or exceeding this age. As of 2011, the median age of Corps hydropower facilities was 47 years, and 90% of Corps projects are 34 years or older.[24] Although hydroelectric generation is highly variable and depends on a number of factors, some have observed that nationwide, generation at Corps units has fallen over the last decade. According to the Corps, from 2000 to 2008 generation at its facilities fell from 71,600 GWH in 2000 to 61,700 GWH in 2008. The extent to which this trend is due to aging infrastructure in uncertain; however, some contend age is a factor in declining generation.[25] Relative to national generation totals, the

---

[20] Douglas G. Hall and Kelly S. Reeves, *A Study of United States Hydroelectric Plant Ownership*, Idaho National Laboratory, INL/EXT-06-11519, Idaho Falls, ID, June 2006, (hereinafter referred to as "Hall and Reeves"). http://www.inl.gov/technicalpublications/Documents/3374828.pdf.

[21] Hall and Reeves, p vi.

[22] Corps Hydropower Outlook, p. 9.

[23] U.S. Congress, House Committee on Natural Resources, Subcommittee on Water and Power, *Statement of Michael Ensch, Chief of Operations, U.S. Army Corps of Engineers, Investment in Small Hydropower Prospects of Expanding Low-Impact and Affordable Hydropower Generation in the West*, 111th Cong., 2nd sess., July 29, 2010, p. 2. Hereinafter referred to as "Ensch."

[24] Corps Hydropower Outlook, p. 2.

[25] Corps Hydropower Outlook, p. 9. Availability of water, including the lack of water in certain hydrological conditions and instream flow requirements, are some of the other factors that may account for decreased generation.

Corps contribution to total hydropower generation decreased from approximately 27% of total production in 2000 to 24% of total production in 2008.[26]

In addition to overall declining generation trends, the delivery of Corps hydroelectric power is also an issue connected to aging infrastructure. That is, unit availability is down because of maintenance and repairs.[27] According to the Corps, many of its hydropower assets have fallen below the generally accepted hydropower industry goal of 95% unit availability. Unit availability at Corps dams has fallen to the point where no Corps division is meeting the 95% target, while at the same time, the total hours of "forced outages" have grown.[28]

Concerns related to aging infrastructure have resulted in internal reviews of the Corps hydropower program and recommendations for ways to improve Corps hydropower operations. The Corps has conducted preliminary reviews of foregone benefits associated with its aging hydropower infrastructure under its Hydropower Modernization Initiative (HMI). The first phase of this initiative, completed in 2010, evaluated several facilities that the Corps had identified as requiring rehabilitation. The Corps concluded that modernization of six "critical needs" projects could produce 341 GWH in additional electricity, or an average increase in production of approximately 8% per plant.[29] The cost for these upgrades would be approximately $600 million. The second phase of the HMI looked at facilities outside the Federal Columbia River Power System (i.e., projects not funded by the Bonneville Power Administration, or BPA) and concluded that if the Corps took no action to modernize the 54 units not financed by BPA, it would forego potential revenues of approximately $7 billion over a 20 year horizon.[30] Costs for the upgrades necessary to avoid the aforementioned losses were estimated at $3.7 billion.

Nonfederal Development at Corps Facilities

Besides federal investment and development, nonfederal development of hydropower at Corps sites is also permissible under certain circumstances. According to the Corps, as of 2010 there were 90 nonfederal power units at Corps dams with a total capacity of .003 GW.[31] Such development requires a Federal Energy Regulatory Commission (FERC) license and a Corps Section 408 permit, which authorizes the nonfederal use of a federal facility.[32] The Corps and FERC signed a Memorandum of Understanding (MOU) in March 2011 to coordinate the regulatory review; among other things, the MOU indicates that the Corps will conduct its regulatory review concurrently to the FERC process to the extent possible.[33]

---

[26] CRS analysis of Corps and EIA data. Again, this calculation does not account for water availability in different regions of the country, which has the ability to effect the Corps contribution to overall generation.

[27] "Unit availability" is generally defined as the amount of time (or in this case, percentage of time) a unit is available to produce electricity, regardless of whether or not it is operated.

[28] Corps Hydropower Outlook, p. 10.

[29] Ensch, p. 3.

[30] Montgomery, Watson, Harza, *Phase II Needs and Opportunities Evaluation and Ranking, Reconnaissance Hydroelectric Assessment Plants Life Extensions and Upgrades, Cumberland River Basin.* Report prepared for the U.S. Army Corps of Engineers Nashville District, Contract No. W912P5-06-D-0008-0004.

[31] Ensch, p. 3.

[32] 33 U.S.C. §408.

[33] Corps and FERC, *Memorandum of Understanding between United States Army Corps of Engineers and the Federal Energy Regulatory Commission on Non-Federal Hydropower Projects*, http://www.ferc.gov/legal/maj-ord-reg/mou/mou-usace.pdf.

Bureau of Reclamation Projects

Reclamation is the second largest producer of hydroelectric power in the United States. Reclamation operates in the 17 western states, and 11 of these states have Reclamation hydropower facilities.[34] As part of its mission to facilitate settlement of the West through water resources development, Reclamation built numerous projects that included facilities to impound water to provide water supply for irrigation and municipal use and to capture floodwaters. Reclamation also constructed hydropower units at some of these facilities, in part to finance project construction for these other purposes.[35] Reclamation constructed some of these units in the early part of the 20th century, and significantly increased its hydropower production during World War II to meet wartime production demands.

> ### Federal Dam Removal and Hydropower
>
> Interest in dam removal for ecosystem and species restoration and recreational purposes is a controversial issue, especially when the dam is producing hydroelectric power. Congress becomes involved as proposals for federal dam removal are considered for authorization and appropriations, as well as in the ongoing implementation of some dam removal projects. There are a few federal facilities with hydropower units where dam removal has been debated. The most controversial case for the Corps is the proposed removal of four Corps locks and dams on the lower Snake River (WA). These facilities have 3GW of capacity (approximately 12% of total Corps capacity) and average annual generation of 7,800 GWH. They also support navigation of the river by commercial barges. The interest in dam removal derives from efforts to restore fish passage for migratory salmon and species listed under the Endangered Species Act. As of 2012, Congress had not acted on proposals for removal of these dams; removal proponents continue to press for these actions.

Reclamation operates 194 generating units at 58 projects, with total capacity of 14.8 GW, or about 16% of the Nation's hydropower capacity. Reclamation generates on average 40,000 GWH annually.

There are two tiers of customers for federal hydropower projects. For Reclamation projects, power is first used for project purposes (e.g., pumping of water for irrigation); the remaining power is marketed by one of the Power Marketing Administrations with jurisdiction over the area (Bonneville Power Administration (BPA) or the Western Area Power Administration (WAPA). In turn, the PMAs provide this power for distribution and sale (see below section, "Hydropower Receipts and Federal Power Marketing Administrations"). Receipts from hydropower revenues at Reclamation Facilities are deposited into the Reclamation Fund and are first applied to project repayment costs.[36]

Like the Corps, Reclamation has identified challenges associated with the operation of its facilities. Similar to the Corps, Reclamation's facilities are aging: the majority of Reclamation's hydroelectric dams are 40-60 years old, and as of 2007 the average age of its hydropower facilities was 51 years.[37] Reclamation in 2008 estimated that approximately $1.4 billion is needed to upgrade its hydropower assets.[38] However, unlike the Corps, net generation at Reclamation

---

[34] Reclamation operates hydropower projects in the following states (in order of generation capacity): Washington, Oregon, California, Arizona, Nevada, Idaho, Montana, Wyoming, Utah, Colorado, and New Mexico.

[35] Although the Reclamation Act of 1902 was the original statute authorizing construction of Reclamation projects. The Reclamation Service (later renamed the Bureau of Reclamation) was first authorized to develop hydropower resources in the Town Site and Power Development Act of 1906 (34 Stat 116). The Fact Finders' Act of 1924 (43 Stat 701) later authorized the use of hydropower revenues as a credit to construction charges of a project.

[36] For more on the Reclamation Fund, see CRS Report R41844, *The Reclamation Fund A Primer*, by Charles V. Stern.

[37] U.S. Bureau of Reclamation, Reclamation-Wide Power Profile. Available at http://www.usbr.gov/power/data/recl-wid.pdf.

[38] Statement of Robert W. Johnson, U.S. Congress, Senate Committee on Energy and Natural Resources, Subcommittee on Water and Power, *Statement of Robert W. Johnson, Hearing on Reclamation's Aging Infrastructure*, (continued...)

facilities has remained somewhat constant over the last 10 years, and Reclamation has stated that its project performance is generally favorable compared to most industry benchmarks.[39]

Reclamation has also studied the potential gains associated with upgrades to its hydropower facilities. However, the potential for additional development at Reclamation facilities appears to be considerably less than that for Corps facilities. In a 2010 study, Reclamation concluded that significant upgrades were only feasible at 10 of its 58 facilities, and would increase Reclamation's total capacity by .067 GW, or less than less than 1%.[40]

Nonfederal Development at Reclamation Facilities

Nonfederal hydropower facilities at existing Reclamation projects is permitted by Reclamation. The process is accomplished through either: 1) a FERC license (for projects not authorized for hydropower); or 2) through a process managed by Reclamation known as the Lease of Power Privilege Process (for projects authorized for hydropower, but not developed). As of 2010, Reclamation reported this type of development at 47 sites which provided capacity of over .46 GW.[41] According to Reclamation, whichever of these processes is used, power development must not conflict with the purposes for which Congress authorized the original Reclamation project, and must not affect the structural and operational integrity of the project. Furthermore, the development must not have significant adverse environmental, cultural, or historical impacts.[42]

Hydropower Receipts and Federal Power Marketing Administrations

The federal government operates four Power Marketing Administrations—Bonneville Power Administration (BPA) in the Pacific Northwest, Southeastern Power Administration (SEPA), Southwestern Power Administration (SWPA), and Western Area Power Administration (WAPA).[43] Each is operated as a distinct and self-contained entity within DOE. Among other responsibilities, the PMAs are responsible for marketing surplus power from Corps and Reclamation facilities to their customers.[44] The revenue collected from the sale of this power is deposited into the Treasury.[45] It is used to pay with interest the federal investment in the hydropower facilities. Gross annual revenue returned to the Treasury from power sales of electricity at federal facilities is estimated at approximately $5 billion, and usually amounts to considerably more than the

---

(...continued)

110th Cong., 2nd sess., April 2008.

[39] This statement takes into account "available water" for generation, which Reclamation tracks. For instance, see http://www.usbr.gov/power/data/recl-wid.pdf, p. 6.

[40] Bureau of Reclamation, *Assessment of Potential Capacity Increases at Existing Hydropower Plants*, October 2010, http://www.usbr.gov/power/AssessmentReport/USBRHMICapacityAdditionFinalReportOctober2010.pdf.

[41] U.S. Congress, House Committee on Natural Resources, Subcommittee on Water and Power, *Statement Michael Conner, Commission, Bureau of Reclamation, Hearing on Investment in Small Hydropower Prospects of Expanding Low-Impact and Affordable Hydropower Generation in the West*, 111th Cong., 2nd sess., July 29, 2010.

[42] For more information on the program, see http://www.usbr.gov/uc/power/progact/nonfedpwr.html.

[43] For more information, see CRS Report R41960, *Federal Agency Authority to Contract for Electric Power and Renewable Energy Supply*, by Anthony Andrews.

[44] Some of the PMAs also own and operate transmission lines associated with these facilities.

[45] Revenues from most hydropower receipts are deposited into the General Fund of the Treasury, although as previously discussed, some hydropower receipts at Reclamation projects are credited to the Reclamation Fund.

budgets for hydropower and related operations and maintenance (O&M) for the Corps and Reclamation.

The Flood Control Act of 1944 requires that the PMAs produce power "at the lowest possible rate consistent with sound business practices."[46] This means that the PMAs typically sell power at a lower cost than investor-owned utilities (whose purpose is to provide a financial return to investors). This rate-setting policy was established to encourage regional economic development and appropriate use of federal assets. Some have pointed out that current PMA policies result in long-term, low-cost contracts that do not take into consideration major O&M upgrades and replacement, and are therefore artificially lower than the true cost needed to maintain these facilities.[47]

Federal Hydropower Revenues and Fish Mitigation

Revenue that is collected from hydropower customers is a significant source of the funding for fish mitigation activities in some basins, such as the Columbia River basin. In the mid-2000s, BPA used roughly $260 million annually from hydropower revenues for salmon recovery and mitigation efforts; this represented roughly ha f of the annual federal funding for Columbia River Endangered Species Act compliance efforts.

Source: Statement of Robert W. Johnson, Commissioner, Bureau of Reclamation, Department of the Interior before the House Committee on Natural Resources, June 12, 2008.

Opportunities and Challenges

Hydropower generation at federal facilities has occurred since the early 20th century and is well established. These projects have provided low-cost power to many, but also have associated environmental costs. As previously noted, several recent studies have noted the potential for increases in federal hydropower, both through efficiency gains and through development of nonfederal power at federal sites. For instance, Corps and Reclamation staff have estimated that approximately 2.4 GW of new capacity (i.e., an increase of as much as 7% on top of existing federal capacity) may be technically feasible to add through additional hydropower development or refurbishment of existing facilities. While fully realizing this potential would likely depend on a number of economic and environmental factors, most agree there is some potential for additional development.

However, challenges to future production and development persist. At Corps facilities in particular, hydroelectric production is facing a number of challenges. A common issue, cited by many, is aging federal hydropower infrastructure, which is often tied to decreasing generation and increases in forced outages of hydropower units. The Federal Government is faced with limited options for dealing with these issues. Financing major upgrades and expansions of federal hydropower facilities beyond immediate maintenance needs is difficult to accomplish without congressional appropriations and, in some cases, authorizations. Construction of new projects also faces challenges. As with expansions and upgrades, new federal developments are dependent upon congressional actions. Other challenges for hydropower at or on federal facilities include

- Environmental operating restrictions in place to protect species that would otherwise be harmed by these projects;

- Uncertain and variable hydrologic conditions (e.g., precipitation and runoff patterns related to climate variability and change);

---

[46] 16 U.S.C. §825s.

[47] Corps Hydropower Outlook, p. 39.

- Limited operational flexibility (e.g., limits derived from congressional authorization and carefully negotiated operating manuals); and

- Demand for water by other competing uses (e.g., municipal water supply and navigation).

Nonfederal Hydropower

Nonfederal hydropower projects can be privately owned or publicly owned, and may or may not be located at a federal site. They differ from federal projects primarily in that they are subject to regulation stemming from their licensing by FERC. According to U.S. Energy Information Administration (EIA) data, roughly 1,245 nonfederal hydropower plants generated 147,400 GWh of net electricity generation in 2010.[48] The amount generated constitutes roughly 57% of total electricity generated from hydropower and roughly 4% of total U.S. electricity in 2010.[49]

In addition to the general advantages and disadvantages of hydropower discussed earlier in this report, nonfederal projects have unique benefits. For example, some argue that nonfederal projects are more likely to receive regular maintenance and major upgrades than federal projects, since the plant owner has a financial incentive to generate as much electricity as possible. On the other hand, drawbacks of nonfederal projects generally mirror those of federal projects (e.g., initial high capital costs, environmental concerns, regulatory requirements). An additional drawback of nonfederal projects is the length of time required to obtain state and federal approval. Some surmise that any increase in hydropower generation is most likely to come from nonfederal projects because, as described earlier, federal projects face hurdles that could prevent them from adding substantial generation capacity quickly, with the major barrier being federal financing for major upgrades and expansions.

Federal Energy Regulatory Commission

FERC licenses the construction and operation of nonfederal hydropower projects.[50] It has the exclusive authority to license new nonfederal hydropower projects, relicense existing projects and provide oversight for all ongoing projects, and it has a role in the decommissioning of projects.[51]

---

[48] Energy Information Administration, *2010 December EIA-923 Monthly Time Series File*, http://www.eia.gov/cneaf/ electricity/page/eia906_920.html. The amount generated is enough to power roughly 13 million "average" homes, based on EIA 2010 data for the average annual electricity consumption (11,496 kWh, or 11.5 MWh)) for a U.S. residential utility customer.

[49] CRS calculations do not include pumped storage.

[50] Three divisions under the FERC Office of Energy Projects (OEP) administer the hydropower responsibilities of the Commission—the Division of Hydropower Licensing (DHL), the Division of Hydropower Administration and Compliance (DHAC), and the Division of Dam Safety and Compliance (DDSC). DHL is responsible for case management and order preparation for applications for licenses, relicensing, exemptions, major amendment of licenses, 5MW exemptions, and license surrender of constructed projects. DHL is also responsible for the preparation of NEPA documents (e.g., environmental assessments and environmental impact statements) and pre-filing collaborative work. DHAC is primarily responsible for reviewing and ensuring compliance by owners of hydropower projects with the conditions specified in their licenses and exemptions. DDSC is responsible for construction, operation, exemption, prelicense, and environmental and public use inspections; engineering evaluations and studies; independent consultant report reviews; emergency action plan development and testing; engineering guidelines development; and interagency/industry committee participation.

[51] In addition to issuing licenses, FERC reports that it has the legal authority to deny a new license at the time of (continued...)

FERC was granted this authority under the Federal Power Act of 1935 (16 U.S.C. 791-828c). FERC may issue a license for a hydroelectric project that

- is located on navigable waters of the United States;

- occupies public lands or reservations of the United States;

- utilizes surplus water or water power from a U.S. government dam; or

- is located on a body of water over which Congress has Commerce Clause jurisdiction, for which project construction occurred on or after August 26, 1935, and which affects interstate or foreign commerce.[52]

FERC reports that the 1,600 projects it regulates at over 2,500 dams represent 54 GW of hydropower capacity, or more than half of all U.S. hydropower.[53] FERC has issued a license for 1,017 projects and has given an exemption for 624 additional projects.[54] Licenses are typically issued for 50 years, but if the relicensing process is underway, an annual license is issued. A 2012 CRS analysis of existing FERC license expiration dates suggests that 47 licensed projects (4.6%) are set to expire between January 2010 and December 2015, 46 licensed projects (4.5%) are set to expire between January 2012 and December 2016, and 90 licensed projects (8.8%) are set to expire between January 2017 and December 2021.[55] No expiration dates are provided by FERC for exemptions, as they are issued in perpetuity.[56]

As an independent agency, FERC's job with respect to hydropower is to license and oversee projects and not necessarily to encourage or discourage additional hydropower development, or to quicken the rate at which projects come online. FERC has worked with stakeholders, as directed by Congress, to streamline its application process. FERC now has three licensing processes that applicants may use to apply for a new license or relicense—the Traditional Licensing Process (TLP), the Alternative Licensing Process (ALP), and the Integrated Licensing Process(ILP).[57] In July 2005, the ILP became the default licensing process (see **Appendix**).[58]

(...continued)

relicensing. For more on license denial, dam removal, and dam decommissioning, see CRS Report RL33480, *Dam Removal Issues, Considerations, and Controversies*, by Nic Lane; and Federal Energy Regulatory Commission, "Project Decommissioning at Relicensing; Policy Statement," 60 *Federal Register* 339-356, Jan. 4, 1995.

[52] 16 U.S.C §817.

[53] Testimony of Jeff C. Wright, in U.S. Congress, Senate Committee on Energy and Natural Resources, *Full Committee Hearing To Hear Testimony on S. 629, S. 630, and Title I, Subtitle D of the American Clean Energy Leadership Act of 2009*, 111th Cong., 1st sess., March 31, 2011.

[54] A list of licenses and exemptions is available at the FERC Hydropower website: http://www.ferc.gov/industries/ hydropower.asp. Reasons for the difference in the number of nonfederal facilities (roughly 1,600 according to FERC and roughly 1,245 according to EIA) are unclear.

[55] According to a Nov. 2010 letter submitted to Congress by FERC, licenses for over 50 hydroelectric projects have expired or will expire between January 2010 and December 2015. See http://www.ferc.gov/about/strat-docs/fy09-an-rpt.pdf.

[56] Some projects are granted an exemption which exempts the project from licensing. FERC offers two types of exemptions: small hydropower and conduits. For more information on exemptions, see http://www.ferc.gov/industries/ hydropower/gen-info/licensing/exemptions.asp.

[57] For background on licensing processes, see CRS Report RL31903, *Relicensing of Nonfederal Hydroelectric Projects Background and Procedural Reform Issues*, by Nic Lane.

[58] Applicants may petition to use either the ALP or the TLP based on anticipated costs, level of complexity and controversy related to licensing, and other factors.

Several factors may affect FERC's ability to keep up with the license application workload. Staff must spend time informing potential applicants about what license they qualify for, and must ensure compliance with various laws. Also, obtaining a FERC license can involve roughly a dozen federal and state agencies, and in some cases the application period may last for six years or more.[59] Federal and state agencies that are consulted during the process may not always adhere to the requisite time frames. For instance, a 2001 FERC report to Congress on hydroelectric license policies notes that a common reason license applications are delayed is untimely receipt of state water quality certification under the Clean Water Act.[60] Testimony by a FERC representative delivered at a 2011 congressional hearing further expresses FERC's perspective:

> Project developers and other stakeholders, not the Commission, in most instances play the leading role in determining project success and whether the regulatory process will be short or long, simple or complex.
>
> To the extent that a proposed project, even one of small size, raises concerns about water use and other environmental issues, it may be difficult for the Commission to quickly process an application. It is important to remember that the small capacity of a proposed project does not necessarily mean that the project has only minor environmental impacts.[61]

Opportunities and Challenges

In many respects, nonfederal projects face the same challenges and opportunities as federal projects. Both must consider power generation, environmental concerns, and surrounding community issues (e.g., safety, recreation). Furthermore, hydropower projects can come with issues associated with power grid connection and transmission. However, there are some issues unique to nonfederal projects such as satisfying FERC licensing requirements.

Many contend that generation capacity at nonfederal projects could be expanded if the financial incentives were adequate. Congress may consider whether to modify tax incentives or provide other subsidies, and could further examine the role of FERC. Environmental costs and impacts associated with expansion could also be considered.

Challenges unique to nonfederal hydropower projects generally emerge from the regulatory framework. Some regulatory challenges involve the issuance and renewal of licenses in a timely manner, and the adequacy of the federal workforce to oversee the license and exemption process. Other challenges include community opposition, market demand fluctuations, and data submission and analysis to better assess production capability. For some time there has been criticism of FERC's handling of its licensing responsibilities, much of which centers on the assertion that the full potential of nonfederal hydropower is not being delivered because of

---

[59] An initial consultation contact list is available for each state, with information on federal, state, and regional agencies and more, at http://www.ferc.gov/industries/hydropower/enviro/consultlist.aspx. For an account of the changes to hydropower license processes over time, see CRS Report RL31903, *Relicensing of Nonfederal Hydroelectric Projects Background and Procedural Reform Issues*, by Nic Lane.

[60] FERC, Report on Hydroelectric Licensing Policies, Procedures, and Regulations Comprehensive Review and Recommendations Pursuant to Section 603 of the Energy Act of 2000, May 2001, http://www.ferc.gov/legal/maj-ord-reg/land-docs/ortc_final.pdf.

[61] Testimony of Jeff C. Wright, in U.S. Congress, Senate Committee on Energy and Natural Resources, *Full Committee Hearing to hear testimony on S. 629, S. 630, and Title I, Subtitle D of the American Clean Energy Leadership Act of 2009*, 111th Cong., 1st sess., March 31, 2011.

licensing delays. Some argue that additional generation capacity from hydropower would be possible if FERC's licensing process was less of a barrier, specifically with respect to the amount of information needed to apply for a license and the time it takes to acquire a license. One issue of particular concern to some stakeholders is the requirement that agencies review and provide "mandatory conditions" to protect fish and other resources as part of the licensing process.[62] Others argue that the licensing process needs to be comprehensive, allowing impacted parties adequate time to review the application and offer comment because, once approved, licenses are valid for 30 to 50 years.

Although the challenges for nonfederal projects are significant, there may be opportunities to overcome or minimize the significance of the barriers mentioned above. For example, energy legislation incorporating a federal renewable electricity or clean energy standard that includes hydropower or a price on carbon could absolve some market anxiety and lead to rapid large-scale investments in new nonfederal projects. Moreover, energy efficiency measures and technological advancements could spur additional generation at existing projects.

Other Nonfederal Hydropower Issues

Other pressing issues associated with nonfederal hydropower include its treatment in state renewable portfolio standards, annual charges by FERC for federal lands transferred with a power site classification, and residential and commercial development on the shoreline of FERC-regulated hydropower projects. These issues, which are discussed below, may have an indirect impact on the progress of hydropower to meet current and future energy demand.

Role of Hydropower in Renewable Electricity Standards

Some in Congress are interested in strategies that could support more domestic renewable energy production. One proposed strategy is a federal renewable electricity standard (RES) or clean energy standard (CES) (e.g., S. 2146), which could require certain retail electricity suppliers to provide a minimum percentage of the electricity they sell from renewable energy sources or other resources.[63] While a federal RES has yet to be established, many states have created a renewable portfolio standard (RPS)—essentially the same as an RES but carried out at the state level. As of March 2012, there were 29 states and the District of Columbia and Puerto Rico that had an RPS.[64]

The inclusion of hydropower in state standards is not uniform, with each state setting its own criteria. The state standards generally have similar intents, but differ in how they achieve their goals. For example, many have different yearly targets and eligibility requirements for renewable sources. Some state standards include hydropower, but almost always with conditions (e.g., allowing only new hydro projects that have a capacity of 10 MW or less and do not require a new

---

[62] For more information on the licensing process, see **Appendix**. For more information on mandatory conditions, see Federal Energy Regulatory Commission, U.S. Department of Interior, and U.S. Department of Commerce, et al., *Interagency Task Force Report on Agency Recommendations, Conditions, and Prescriptions Under Part I of the Federal Power Act*, December 2000, http://www.ferc.gov/industries/hydropower/indus-act/itf/fpa_final.pdf.

[63] For more information, see CRS Report R42522, *Clean Energy Standard Summary and Analysis of S. 2146*, by Phillip Brown, CRS Report R41797, *Clean Energy Standard Potential Qualifying Energy Sources*, coordinated by Kelsi Bracmort, and CRS Report R41493, *Options for a Federal Renewable Electricity Standard*, by Richard J. Campbell.

[64] DSIRE, *Quantitative RPS Data Project*, October 2011, http://www.dsireusa.org/rpsdata/index.cfm.

---

dam, allowing only existing hydro projects of 30 MW or less, excluding pumped storage, only including incremental production at existing facilities). Furthermore, the location and delivery requirements for the electricity generated differs for state standards, with a handful of states having caveats for "geographic eligibility" concerns for hydro projects.[65]

Federal Power Act Section 24 Power Site Reservations

The "power site reservation" under Section 24 of the Federal Power Act has been the subject of a number of administrative disputes over the years.[66] Power site classification is the classification of public lands that have potential value for water power development. Traditionally, the U.S. Geological Survey (USGS) has had the authority to classify the lands as having potential value for water power development (i.e., power site classification), FERC has jurisdiction over the power value on the lands, and BLM has certain management jurisdiction over the surface and subsurface resources, but not the power value. Once land is assigned a power site classification, this classification remains with the land. The classification is not extinguished if the land has been transferred out of federal ownership, although there is a process to extinguish the classification.

An administrative dispute associated with power site classification is that hydropower projects on land transferred from federal ownership to state ownership are still subject to annual fees if the land has a power site classification.[67] According to FERC, annual charges are still required for federal lands that were transferred with a power site classification because the classification remains with the land and the United States still has the right to obtain power from this land.[68] FERC does not keep a record of the number of lands transferred with a power site classification.

Hydroelectric Power and Shoreline Management Plans

Controversies over property rights in areas near hydropower facilities have drawn attention to the FERC "Shoreline Management Plan" (SMP) process. An SMP governs the use and occupancy of the project reservoir shoreline for activities not related to hydropower production. Recent FERC orders proposing to limit acceptable use and occupancy near hydroelectric facilities, including potential interference with existing recreational and other structures, have drawn the ire of nearby communities (see **Appendix**). With an SMP, FERC is trying to ensure that waterfront development along the shoreline of hydropower projects does not have an adverse impact on project operations, public safety, commercial navigation, and other interests. In recent years, property owners along some reservoirs have complained when reservoirs are drawn down to produce power. Such conflicts between shorelines uses can be especially acute during droughts.

[65] Union of Concerned Scientists, *Renewable Electricity Standards Toolkit*, http://go.ucsusa.org/cgi-bin/RES/state_standards_search.pl?template=main.

[66] Section 24 (16 U.S.C. §818) establishes that when FERC licenses a hydropower facility on federal land, it reserves lands associated with that facility for the federal government, and that if and when such lands are later transferred by the federal government, the government reserves the ability to continue to regulate the hydroelectric facility.

[67] In November 2011, FERC issued a proposal to revise the methodology for assessing annual charges for the use of federal lands by hydropower projects. Federal Energy Regulatory Commission, "Annual Charges for Use of Government Lands," 76 *Federal Register* 72134-72142, November 22, 2011.

[68] Personal communication with FERC Office of the General Counsel, January 31, 2012. Annual charges for hydropower projects allow FERC to recover costs incurred in the performance of its regulatory responsibilities. Information on annual charges, including FERC's proposal to revise the methodology for calculating rental rates for the use of federal lands by hydropower projects is available at http://www.ferc.gov/industries/hydropower/annual-charges.asp.

The source of FERC's authority to require SMPs and to enforce their terms on hydropower license applicants is primarily found in Sections 10(a)(1) and 4(e) of the FPA.[69] Section 10(a)(1) directs FERC to issue hydropower licenses that include a "comprehensive plan for improving or developing a waterway or waterways for the use or benefit of interstate or foreign commerce, for the improvement and utilization of waterpower development, for the adequate protection mitigation, and enhancement of fish and wildlife … and for other beneficial public uses." Shoreline management plans are one way that FERC ensures that hydroelectric facilities that it permits satisfy these requirements. The requirement that FERC-permitted hydropower facilities file and abide by SMPs is not in the Federal Power Act (FPA).[70] In fact, the phrase "shoreline management plan" does not appear anywhere in the U.S. Code. The only reference to SMPs is in the titles of the *Code of Federal Regulations* as a requirement that existing licensees include their SMPs in their pre-application filing for renewal of the license.[71]

Within this broad statutory framework, FERC decides on a case-by-case basis whether an SMP is warranted for a proposed hydropower licensee. On occasion an applicant has submitted a proposed SMP without prompting. In some cases, FERC determined an SMP was not needed. Regardless of whether a hydropower licensee is required to submit an SMP, all licensees are required to obtain the property rights needed to satisfy any obligations that may be included in an SMP.

Legislative Questions

Federal Hydropower

What Are Some of the Options to Address Aging Hydropower Infrastructure at Existing Federal Hydropower Projects?

As previously discussed, declining generation trends at federal facilities have been tied to aging infrastructure and the need for funds to replace and/or upgrade this infrastructure. Several policy options have previously been proposed to deal with aging federal hydropower infrastructure. Some of these options are specific to the Corps or Reclamation, while others could generally apply to both agencies. All of these options have budgetary costs in one form or another. Some of the options commonly mentioned include

- **Increase federal funding for hydropower upgrades and/or modernization initiatives within annual appropriations process**. This option would maintain the status quo practice of funding hydropower upgrades within existing discretionary budget allocations, albeit at increased levels or over a different timetable. Some point out that increased funding in annual appropriations is unrealistic in the current budgetary climate.

- **Utilize alternative funding mechanisms to finance hydropower upgrades**. Some have proposed alternative funding mechanisms that fall outside of the

---

[69] 16 U.S.C. §803(a)(1).

[70] 16 U.S.C. §792 *et seq.*

[71] 18 C.F.R. §5.6.

regular appropriations process, such as an infrastructure bank or some form of private sector contracting vehicle (such as Energy Savings Performance Contracts, or ESPCs).[72] Advocates argue that these funding mechanisms could increase hydropower production without requiring annual appropriations. However, utilizing these alternative programs to fund federal projects typically entails "up-front" budgetary costs, especially if they entail federal backing or guarantee future federal spending in the form of project revenues.

- **Increase rates to re-coup "full" costs of operations and maintenance (including major upgrades) and/or institute new user charges to pay for upgrades.** Some argue that rates charged by the PMAs should be increased to recover the costs for major infrastructure upgrades. Congress could alter existing law to allow for these increased rates. However, any practice that results in increased rates for PMA customers may be viewed negatively by customers and some Members of Congress.

- **Privatize federally owned dams through divestiture of assets.** One option sometimes raised is the potential to privatize federally owned hydropower assets, thereby relieving the federal government of its operation and maintenance responsibilities and putting these dams in the hands of other interests, who might better afford to invest in facility upgrades that would increase generation. However, private entities might also increase electricity rates to achieve greater revenues and repay investments in these projects.

- **Allow customers to commit future power revenues to pay for major upgrades to federal facilities.** Some would prefer that those entities who benefit from federal hydropower upgrades be allowed to directly finance these upgrades by redirecting funds that would otherwise flow to the Treasury for these projects. Some PMAs, including BPA, already have some form of this authority, and some advocate for extending it to the other PMAs.[73] There would likely be a budgetary cost to allowing for these receipts to be directed anywhere other than the General Treasury.

What Are Some of the Current Data Gaps Related to Federal Hydropower?

Although a number of the studies previously mentioned in this report collected data on federal hydropower resources, several data gaps have been identified. For instance, one study identified a data gap on the value of ancillary benefits from federal hydropower operations.[74] Ancillary benefits, such as the ability to suddenly increase hydropower production when power is needed (and/or other sources are not available), have the potential to boost the stability and resilience of the nation's power system.[75] However, the role and value that federal hydropower sources

---

[72] More information on ESPCs is available at http://www1.eere.energy.gov/femp/financing/espcs.html. Currently, federal hydroelectric projects are ineligible for ESPCs.

[73] Specifically, Congress provided BPA with "self-financing" authority in 1974 (P.L. 93-454) by establishing a separate fund in the Treasury, the Bonneville Fund, in which BPA deposits and manages its revenues. The fund allows for BPA to enter into multi-year commitments. BPA also has the authority to borrow from the Treasury; it must repay these loans with interest at market rates.

[74] Corps Hydropower Outlook, p. 51.

[75] Another ancillary benefit is hydropower's ability to restart electric power systems in the event of a blackout; this is known as "black start."

currently provide or could provide through ancillary benefits has not been well documented. Additionally, although the Bureau of Reclamation has investigated the economic feasibility of uprating and capacity additions at its facilities, the Corps has not published a similar study. Other gaps related to availability of downscaled climate data of sufficient quality to inform operations of hydropower facilities are a source of ongoing controversy for federal projects.[76]

How Does Uncertainty Affect Operations of Federal Projects?

Uncertainty, in the form of natural climate variability and other related changes, has affected water resources in the past and may affect how much and when water is available for hydroelectric generation in the future. Both the Corps and Reclamation have found that operations of federal hydropower infrastructure will need to be altered due to climate change.[77] Federal facilities are often operated based on procedures set out in operating manuals, which are commonly put together based on past trends and the assumption of "stationarity" (i.e., the idea that future hydrologic trends will be similar to past time periods). Revising these estimates can be difficult, and much uncertainty still exists in the process. Alterations to federal operations are further complicated by existing requirements to meet multiple competing goals in the face of uncertain water conditions. Some stakeholders have questioned whether federal agencies will require greater flexibility in operating existing reservoirs if climate conditions result in changes to weather patterns, less predictability, and more extreme events. In 2009, the Secretary of the Interior, Ken Salazar, issued an order stating that the Department (which has purview over the Bureau of Reclamation) would consider and analyze climate change impacts when undertaking long range planning exercises, but to date the effect of the order on hydropower operations at specific facilities remains unclear.[78]

Nonfederal Hydropower

Should Congress Support Additional Nonfederal Hydropower Projects?

There is a debate about whether more nonfederal hydropower could help to meet current and future electricity demand.[79] Additional hydropower could be less harmful to the environment than fossil-fueled electricity generation projects, if hydropower projects conform to certain standards.[80] Hydropower can also be a flexible source of generation. It can be a baseload energy

---

[76] Joshua H. Viers, "Hydropower Relicensing and Climate Change," *Journal of the American Water Resources Association*, vol. 47, no. 4 (August 2011), pp. 655-661.

[77] For example, see the Corps climate response page at http://corpsclimate.us/responses.cfm. Reclamation research on climate change is compiled at http://www.usbr.gov/climate/SECURE/.

[78] Department of the Interior, *Addressing the Impacts of Climate Change on America's Water, Land, and Other Natural Resources*, Order No. 3289, Washington, DC, September 14, 2009, http://www.doi.gov/whatwedo/climate/cop15/upload/SecOrder3289.pdf.

[79] For a variety of reasons, electricity generation from coal is predicted to be on the decline. The energy source that will make up for lost electricity generation from coal is currently under discussion, but most new capacity additions are expected to be from natural gas generators. Any one energy source or mixture of sources could also be tapped to meet consumer demand.

[80] While hydropower is often viewed as being a clean and renewable source of energy, the environmental costs due to stream flow disruption, particularly effects on fish and wildlife, can be quite high. For example, the Bonneville Power Administration and Reclamation spend hundreds of millions on salmon restoration and mitigation activities associated with federal dams and hydropower facilities. Requiring fish mitigation strategies upfront might avoid costly habitat (continued...)

---

source, meaning that it is readily available, or it can be used for peaking, meaning that it is turned off and on to meet peak demand. On the other hand, there can be environmental concerns, regulatory concerns, and energy terrorism. Congress could decide whether to support additional hydropower development, how much additional development is necessary, and whether the current regulatory environment for nonfederal hydropower is appropriate. Congress could also determine how involved it wants to be with nonfederal hydropower projects. Hydropower as a whole is one of the few remaining energy sources where the federal government owns a significant portion of the projects that generate the bulk of the electricity. Congress could decide that hydropower development of a certain size and scale is an energy resource that no longer requires such large ownership and intervention by the U.S. government, possibly transferring some of those activities and infrastructure to nonfederal entities.

In What Ways Can Additional Power Be Generated from Existing Nonfederal Projects?

Congress could offer support for additional hydropower generation using numerous mechanisms. Congress could choose to assess current federally funded efforts for nonfederal hydropower projects and take action by providing supplementary funds or modifying efforts to ensure that congressional goals are met on schedule.[81] Congress may or may not expand and extend tax credits available for hydropower (e.g., H.R. 3307). Congress may or may not establish a clean energy standard that includes hydropower as an eligible clean energy source (e.g., S. 2146). Congress may or may not amend specific laws to expedite the licensing process for select projects (e.g., H.R. 2842).

What Can Congress Do to Expedite Nonfederal Project Licensing?

Congress may decide to further examine the role FERC should or should not have in nonfederal hydropower regulation. Reasons may include time delays throughout the licensing process, such as those related to gathering input from multiple affected parties and agencies. Others may argue that FERC's role in nonfederal hydropower regulation should continue for safety reasons and because public resources are being used to generate power. If the length of time required for licensing continues to be a concern, Congress could impress upon federal, state, and local agencies involved in the licensing process the need to complete their contributions in a prompt manner. On the other hand, some stakeholders might object if they believe their concerns (e.g., fish, wildlife, recreation, water use, or other impacts) are not being thoroughly vetted. Legislative proposals that address project licensing include S. 629 which would, in part, direct FERC to investigate the feasibility of issuing a license for certain hydropower projects within a two-year period beginning on the date a prefiling licensing is submitted.

(...continued)

mitigation later.

[81] For example, DOE supports conventional hydropower through its water power research and development program. The program's conventional hydropower activities are focused on new technologies, optimization, and siting techniques that might improve combined energy and environmental performance.

Conclusion

If Congress determines that increasing hydropower is a priority, then additional hydropower generation could come from either the public or private sectors or both. It is unclear whether financing to construct, operate, and maintain projects will be a federal priority. The private sector has a sizeable presence in the small hydropower market, which may place the sector in a good position to operate and expand power production. However, there are serious doubts about whether investments in large hydropower projects, by either the public or private sector, are likely to happen soon, owing to economic and geographic constraints,[82] environmental concerns, and public perception. It is possible that other forms of water power (e.g., hydrokinetics, ocean thermal) may one day contribute to the U.S. energy portfolio, but small hydropower is a more likely near-term option.

As Congress considers whether to alter support for hydropower development, it is also dealing with current hydropower infrastructure issues. These issues include aging infrastructure, delayed maintenance, the permitting process, and water availability. Congress may decide to address these concerns in a variety of ways. For example, legislation passed the House in the 112th Congress that would exempt nonfederal projects of 1.5 megawatts or less from certain FERC licensing requirements (i.e., H.R. 2842), and proposed legislation would give tax parity to hydropower projects (e.g., S. 631).[83] Some could argue that hydropower does not need assistance in the form of tax credits because it is an established source and tax credits should be issued to ease the entry of new renewable energy sources to the market or all types of generation should have to compete without federal support. Others could argue that tax credits are needed for hydropower to defray the large capital costs associated with new projects.

Many of the hydropower issues Congress is likely to address in the near term are the same issues it has addressed for some time: operation of federal projects, the permitting process for nonfederal projects, and environmental impacts. The federal government has been responsible for ownership and operation of the bulk of the larger projects. Regular maintenance and upkeep of federal projects has not kept a pace that some would prefer. Also, developers of nonfederal projects would like an easier way to obtain permits and financing for their projects. The nonfederal project permit process has been revised over time in an effort to streamline the process, but still is unacceptable to some.

Hydropower has a long tenure in the electricity market, and its advantages and disadvantages are well documented. However, there are questions for Congress about whether hydropower capacity could or should be increased, and whether that increase should occur at existing projects or by building new projects (including small and low-head hydropower), or both. Other issues affecting conventional hydropower involve the development of nonconventional hydropower technologies, competition from other energy sources (e.g., wind) that are perceived to be more environmentally friendly, and competition from fossil fuel energy sources that may be significantly cheaper (e.g., natural gas).

---

[82] Most of the large, economically feasible generation sites were developed in the 20th century.

[83] Other electricity sources receive tax incentives.

Appendix. FERC Integrated Licensing Process

FERC's Integrated Licensing Process

The Integrated Licensing Process (ILP) was implemented in 2005 to offer a more efficient licensing process.[84] The ILP incorporates elements of the Traditional Licensing Process (TLP) created in 1985 (e.g., deadlines for multiple steps), and the Alternative Licensing Process (ALP) created in 1997 (e.g., focus on early stakeholder involvement). Additionally, the ILP includes a new process for resolving study disputes and requires FERC to participate earlier in the licensing process. FERC indicates that these changes are intended to make the process shorter and more efficient without altering agencies' authorities under the Federal Power Act (16 U.S.C. §791 et al.) or the Clean Water Act (33 U.S.C. §1341) to develop license conditions that protect fish, federal reservations (e.g., national forests, Indian reservations), or rivers' state-designated uses. The ILP differs from the TLP and the ALP in that it is more collaborative than the TLP and more structured than the ALP. Also, the ILP moves FERC's National Environmental Policy Act (NEPA) scoping process from the post-application phase to the pre-application phase in an effort to resolve study disputes early in the licensing process.

Some entities that might be consulted during the licensing process include

- National Marine Fisheries Service (NOAA Fisheries)
- U.S. Fish and Wildlife Service (FWS)
- National Park Service (NPS)
- U.S. Environmental Protection Agency (EPA)
- the federal agency administering any United States lands or facilities to be used or occupied by the project
- any state agency with responsibility for fish, wildlife, and botanical resources, water quality, coastal zone management plan consistency certification, shoreline management, and water resources
- the State Historic Preservation Officer (SHPO) and Tribal Historic Preservation Officer (THPO—if applicable)
- local, state, and regional recreation agencies and planning commissions
- local and state zoning agencies
- any Indian tribe that may be affected by the project
- any potentially affected landowners

---

[84] FERC receives an annual appropriation from Congress to defray its operating costs and recovers 100 percent of this appropriation through the collection of annual charges and filing fees. There are no filing fees for hydropower projects. However, there are annual charges for hydropower projects if the project capacity is greater than 1 5 megawatts (MW). The annual charges for hydropower projects in 2010 totaled nearly $81 million (The total included 2010 actual administrative charges, 2010 actual fix annual charges, and 2010 other federal agency annual charges. http://www.ferc.gov/industries/hydropower/annual-charges.asp).

Applicable laws that might have to be complied with through out the licensing process include

- Section 401 of the Clean Water Act (CWA)

- Endangered Species Act (ESA)

- Magnuson-Stevens Fishery Conservation and Management Act

- Coastal Zone Management Act (CZMA)

- National Historic Preservation Act (NHPA)

- Pacific Northwest Power Planning and Conservation Act (Act)

- Wild and Scenic Rivers and Wilderness Act

Author Contact Information

Kelsi Bracmort
Specialist in Agricultural Conservation and Natural
Resources Policy
kbracmort@crs.loc.gov, 7-7283

Charles V. Stern
Specialist in Natural Resources Policy
cstern@crs.loc.gov, 7-7786

Adam Vann
Legislative Attorney
avann@crs.loc.gov, 7-6978